COUNTRIES IN OUR WORLD

JAPAN
IN OUR WORLD

Jim Pipe

Smart Apple Media

Published by Smart Apple Media
P.O. Box 3263, Mankato, Minnesota 56002

Printed in the United States of America at Corporate Graphics, in North Mankato, Minnesota.

Published by arrangement with the Watts Publishing Group LTD, London.

Library of Congress Cataloging-in-Publication Data
Pipe, Jim, 1966-
Japan in our world / by Jim Pipe.
p. cm. -- (Countries in our world)
Includes bibliographical references and index.
Summary: "Describes the geography, landscape, economy, government, and culture of Japan today and discusses Japan's influence of and relations with the rest of the world"--Provided by publisher.
ISBN 978-1-59920-390-4 (library binding)
1. Japan--Juvenile literature. I. Title.
DS806.P527 2012
952--dc22
201003186

1305
3-2011

9 8 7 6 5 4 3 2 1

Produced for Franklin Watts by
White-Thomson Publishing Ltd
Series consultant: Rob Bowden
Editor: Sonya Newland
Designer: Amy Sparks
Picture researcher: Amy Sparks

Picture Credits
Corbis: 7 (Mikhail Klimentiev/epa), 11 (Franck Robichon/epa), 18 (Pierre Perrin/Sygma), 20 9Franck Robichon/epa), 21 (Xu Xiaolin), 22 (Kim Kyung-Hoon/Reuters), 26 (Kimimasa Myama/epa), 27 (Peter Andrews/Reuters), 29 (Jose Fuste Raga); **Dreamstime:** 9 (Tracey Taylor), 13 (Arena Creative), 16 (Attila Jandi), 17 (Jinlide); **Fotolia:** 25 (Al Teich); **Photolibrary:** 6 (Vidler Vidler); **Shutterstock:** Cover (Hiroshi Ichikawa), 1 (Radu Razvan), 5 (Mypokcik), 8 (Hiroshi Ichikawa), 10 (Tristan Scholze), 12 (Hannahmariah), 14 (Radu Razvan), 15 (Hinochika), 19 (J. Henning Buchholz), 23 (John Leung), 24 (J. Henning Buchholz), 28 (Denis Klimov).

Contents

Introducing Japan

Japan is a country of contrasts. It is one of the world's economic superpowers. However, while it is a modern, developed country, it maintains much of its traditional culture. Its name in Japanese,* Nippon, *means "the source of the sun," which is why Japan is sometimes called the "Land of the Rising Sun."

An Island Nation

Japan lies on the western edge of the Pacific Ocean, off the north-eastern coast of Asia. It consists of four major islands surrounded by approximately 3,900 smaller islands. Put together, these are slightly smaller than the state of California. Despite this, Japan has the tenth-largest population in the world. It is covered in mountains, so most people in Japan live in in towns and cities crammed together on the flat coastal plains. High-rise apartments filled with people are squeezed into these towns and cities. To help solve the problem of overcrowding, land is being reclaimed from the sea.

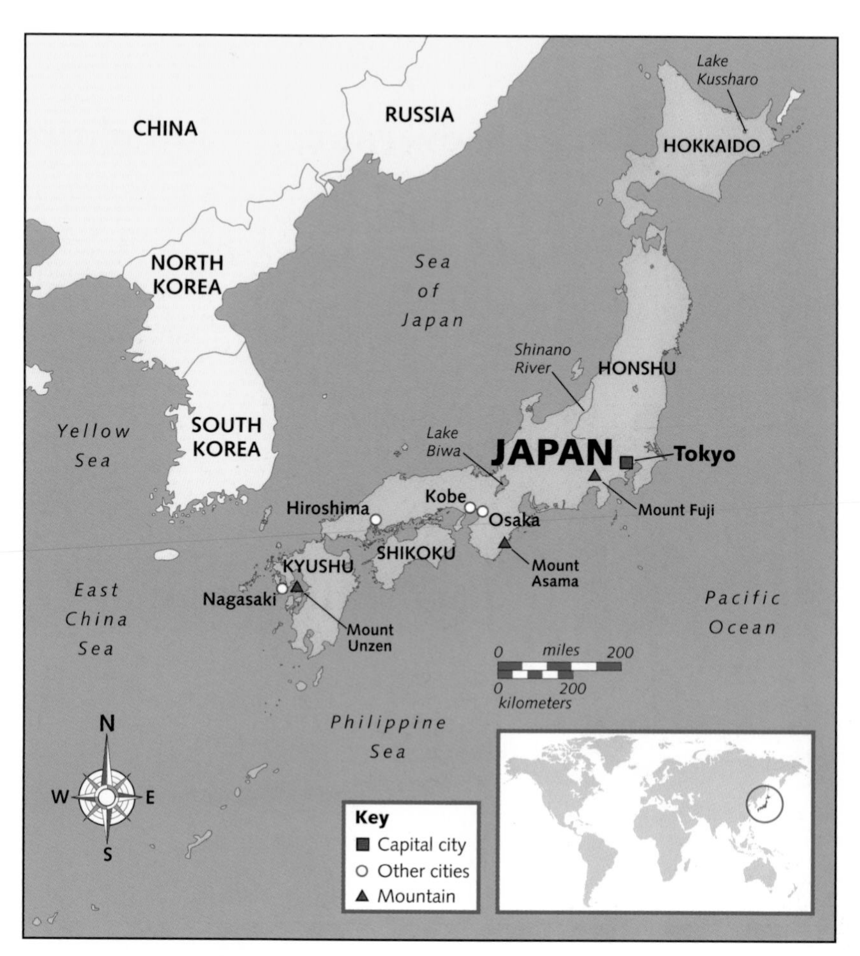

Japan is made up of four main islands and thousands of smaller ones in the Pacific Ocean to the south of the Korean Peninsula and Russia.

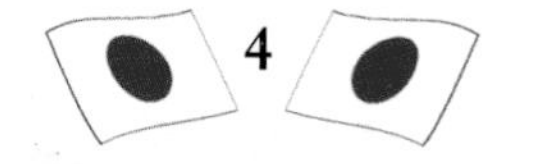

A Global Power

Despite economic difficulties since the mid-1990s, Japan remains the second-richest country in the world. The Japanese people enjoy very high standards of living, and Japan is home to some of the world's most successful companies. Japanese brand names, such as Sony, Toyota, Nintendo, Panasonic, and Canon, are recognized all over the world. Once known for its steel and ship-building industries, Japan is famous today for high-tech goods such as computers, cell phones, game consoles, and music players. It is also the world's fourth-largest exporter and the sixth-largest importer.

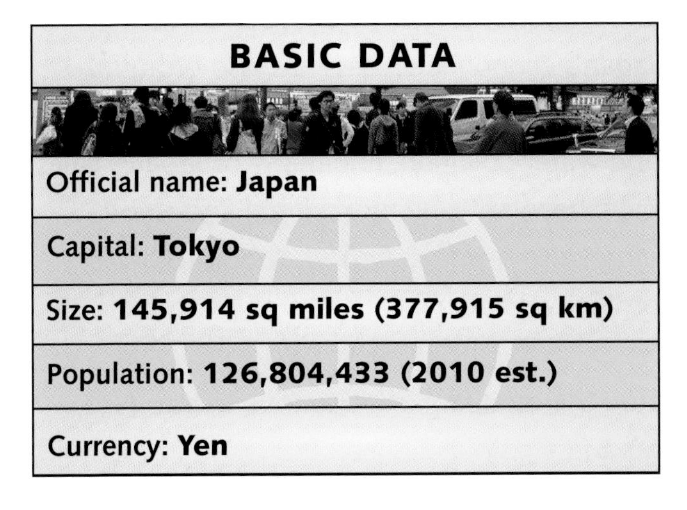

BASIC DATA
Official name: **Japan**
Capital: **Tokyo**
Size: **145,914 sq miles (377,915 sq km)**
Population: **126,804,433 (2010 est.)**
Currency: **Yen**

▼ *In Japan's capital, Tokyo, crowds of people hurry to work during rush hour.*

Environmental Problems

Japan's economic success has also brought problems. The growth of industry has led to air and water pollution, and many of Japan's cities have been affected by acid rain and smog. Japan also needs to find a solution to better protect wildlife habitats. However, to their credit, in the 1970s, new laws were passed to stop the dumping of poisonous waste. Also, Japanese companies lead the world in the development of eco-friendly technology. The hybrid cars built by Toyota and Honda have gas and electric engines that reduce pollution.

THE HOME OF...

Origami

Origami is the art of paper-folding. During the 19th century, Samurai warriors gave gifts decorated with *noshi*, a good-luck token made from paper folded around a strip of dried fish or meat. In time, the designs became more and more intricate. Now, there is even a plan to use special origami planes to test new spacecraft designs.

One of a Kind?

Japanese culture has had a huge impact on the rest of the world—karaoke, computer games, and Pokémon are enjoyed all over the globe. The Japanese have long believed that their country is a special place that few outsiders can understand. When French firms first tried to sell skis to Japan in the 1960s, they were told they wouldn't work as Japanese snow was unique! Today, attitudes are changing, and Japan is more open to foreign influences and competition.

◀ *The growth of industry in Japan has resulted in environmental problems as factories and power plants pump polluting gases into the atmosphere.*

▲ *Japanese prime minister Taro Aso talks with Russian president Dmitri Medvedev during a meeting of the G8 countries in 2009.*

Japan in the World

Japan plays an important role in world politics. It is a member of the G8 group of leading industrial nations, and it hosted the Kyoto agreement on climate change in 1997. It provides a lot of foreign aid to developing countries and lends money to many other nations. Since World War II (1939–45), Japan has had a peaceful foreign policy, but today it feels threatened by the nuclear missile testing in North Korea. Its relations with its powerful neighbors, Russia and China, are very important to the stability of the region.

IT STARTED HERE

Pokémon

Pokémon, the cute cartoon characters that appear in comics, video games, and TV shows, were invented by Satoshi Tajiri in 1996. By 1999, they were a huge hit with children all over the world. Pokémon is a contraction of two words that mean "pocket monsters." Players keep the animated creatures in small electronic gadgets and train them to compete against creatures owned by other players.

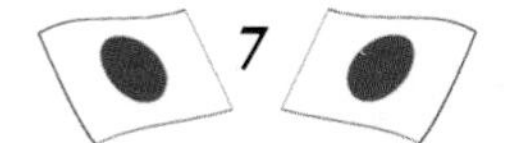

Landscapes and Environment

Japan is a chain of some 3,900 islands in the western Pacific Ocean. Four large islands—Hokkaido, Honshu, Shikoku, and Kyushu—make up 98 percent of its land area. Japan is also a land of volcanoes, mountains, and earthquakes, making it a beautiful, but sometimes dangerous, place to live.

Highs and Lows

Japan's islands were formed by two large pieces of the Earth's crust pushing against each other. Over millions of years, this pressure created the tall mountains and deep valleys that give Japan its distinctive landscape. The tallest peak in Japan is a dormant volcano, Mount Fuji, which is 12,388 ft (3,776 m) high. There are 14 other peaks over 9,843 ft (3,000 m) tall. Three-quarters of Japan is mountainous, with plains and basins covering the remaining area. The largest of these, Kanto Plain, on Honshu island, has an area of over 12,355 sq miles (32,000 sq km).

▼ *Mount Fuji towers over tea plantations. This dormant volcano last erupted in the 18th century.*

IT'S A FACT!

Due to Japan's mountainous countryside, most rivers are fast-flowing. Dams have already been built on many rivers to provide hydroelectric power, but the rivers are also prone to flooding during the rainy season. Over the years, the Japanese government has spent huge amounts of money building complex flood defenses causing few rivers to retain their natural features.

Rivers, Lakes and Seas

Japan is surrounded by sea on all sides. It has a very long coastline—18,486 miles (29,751 km)—shaped by many small peninsulas, bays, and inlets. The Inland Sea separates the islands of Honshu, Shikoku, and Kyushu. Due to Japan's thin shape, its rivers are short. The longest is the Shinano, which flows 228 miles (367 km) into the Sea of Japan. Many of Japan's lakes, such as Lake Biwa and Lake Kussharo, are high up in the craters of extinct volcanoes.

▲ *Lake Kussharo is high up in the mountains of the Akan National Park. As a result, it partly freezes over in winter.*

PLACE IN THE WORLD

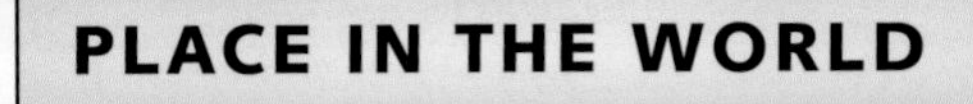

Total area: **145,914 sq miles (377,915 sq km)**

Percentage of world land area: **0.074%**

World ranking: **61st**

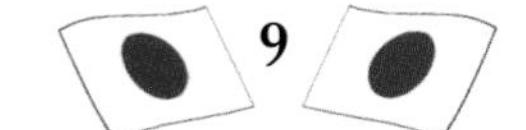

Climate

Like North America, Japan has four seasons: spring, summer, fall, and winter. However, as Japan is 2,051 miles (3,300 km) long, there are big differences in climate from north to south. Hokkaido island in the north has cool, short summers and long, snowy winters. The Ryukyu islands in the south have long, subtropical summers and mild winters. Most rain falls in June to October, when warm winds called monsoons blow from the South Pacific. Storms known as typhoons are common during these months. In 2008, over a million people fled from their homes to avoid landslides and flooding caused by a typhoon.

THE HOME OF...

Garden Art

Japanese gardens are famed for their beauty. Garden design is seen as an art, with rocks, ponds, bridges, and plants such as bonsai trees arranged with great care. Yet this love of order has been disastrous for wildlife in Japan, as very few areas have been left in their natural, wild state.

◀ *To honor the arrival of the cherry blossom in spring, the Japanese hold parties known as* hanami *under the trees.*

Natural Hazards

Japan sits on a very unstable part of the Earth's crust and it has about 75 active volcanoes—roughly 10 percent of the world's total. Forty-three people died in 1991 after Mount Unzen erupted on the southern island of Kyushu. In 2009, a huge eruption by Mount Asama threw ash 1.2 miles (2 km) into the sky. Twenty percent of the world's earthquakes occur in Japan—up to 1,500 a year. In March 2011, a strong earthquake hit the northeast coast. The quake caused a massive tsunami that flooded the coastal towns, causing even more damage. Thousands of people died, and thousands more were left homeless.

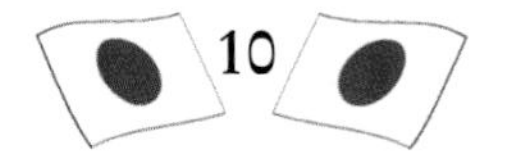

Wildlife in Danger

Japan has traditionally had a wide variety of wildlife due to the range of different habitats. Many species cannot be found anywhere else in the world. However, only a very small percentage of land in Japan is protected by law. The country is also one of the world's biggest traders in endangered species. In addition, tourism has been bad for wildlife as marinas, golf courses, and hotel developments replace natural habitats. As a result, a fifth of Japan's animal and plant species are threatened with extinction, including golden eagles, Asiatic bears, and the Okinawa dugong.

▼ *Although most countries have now banned whaling, it continues in Japan. These men are measuring a beaked whale caught off the Japanese coast.*

IT'S A FACT!

In the mid-19th century, many people in Japan ate whale meat. In the 1990s, most countries agreed to stop killing whales as many species were close to extinction. Japan is one of the few countries against the ban. Its fishing fleet continues to hunt hundreds of whales each year for scientific purposes, and the whale meat is sold to be eaten.

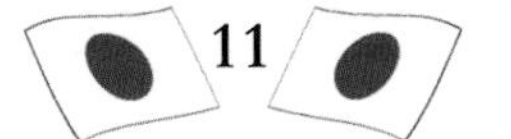

Population and Migration

Almost all Japanese people belong to the same ethnic group, although there are a few minority groups living in Japan. Until the 1980s, the population grew quickly, but since then it has slowed and is now dropping. Despite this, Japanese cities are among the most crowded in the whole world. Twelve Japanese cities have more than one million inhabitants.

IT'S A FACT!

Tokyo is home to over 35 million people and is part of a huge area that includes the neighboring districts of Chiba, Saitama, and Kanagawa. Some districts are populated with over 17,600 people per sq mile (11,000 per sq km), making Tokyo one of the most crowded places on the planet. Not surprisingly, homes in the capital are very small.

▼ *Tokyo is the most populated capital city in the world, and people are often crowded into small apartments in high-rise buildings.*

In the past 20 years, many young Japanese, especially women, have moved to cities such as London and New York in search of a different way of life.

Japanese Around the World

Japanese communities can be found around the world and have helped the spread of Japanese culture. There are about 2.5 million Japanese emigrants, known as *nikkei*, living in countries such as Brazil, Canada, the United States, the United Kingdom, and the Philippines. There is also a small group of Japanese people living in the Caribbean, who come from families that moved there in the 1930s.

Ethnic Minorities

The Ainu were the original settlers of northern Japan. Today, there are around 15,000 Ainu left, living mainly on the island of Hokkaido. The biggest minority group is the Burakumin. They came from an underclass that once did all the jobs thought to be too dirty for everyone else. Today they have the same rights as others, but they still suffer discrimination. There are also around 700,000 Koreans living in Japan. Many come from families that were forced to work in Japanese coal mines and factories during the Japanese occupation of Korea between 1910 and 1945.

GLOBAL LEADER

Life Expectancy

Japan has the highest life expectancy of any country in the world. There are now more people aged over 65 in Japan than children under 14. Many of the oldest people are found in the Amami islands south of Kyushu. Their secret, they say, is an active lifestyle, sea air rich in minerals, and a diet plentiful in seafood, seaweed, and brown sugar.

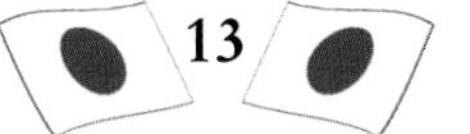

Culture and Lifestyles

Japanese culture is a rich blend of traditional Asian and modern Western influences. Throughout its history, Japan has adopted Chinese writing and ideas, Korean art, and Western technology and clothing. In the last 30 years, there has been a growing interest in Japanese culture in the rest of the world.

▼ *The Japanese reenact famous battles from the past to honor the Samurai warriors.*

IT'S A FACT!

The Japanese warrior class, known as samurai, swore an oath to defend the honor of their name and lord—or die! These knights followed a strict set of rules, known as *Bushido*, "the way of the warrior." The samurai used a range of weapons such as bows and arrows, spears, and guns. Their most famous weapon, as well as their symbol, was the sword.

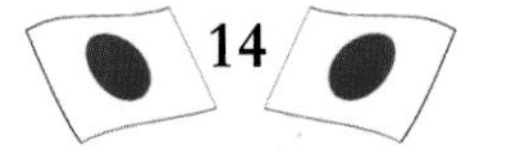

IT STARTED HERE

Novels

***The Tale of Genji* is thought to be the world's first full-length novel. It was written by a Japanese noblewoman named Murasaki Shikibu around AD 1010. She may have based the book on her own experiences at the court of the Japanese emperor.**

Japanese Language

The Japanese have their own language, though different dialects, or *hogen*, are spoken in different parts of the country. The characters used to write Japanese originally came from ancient China. These are called *kanji* and began as pictures. In addition, the Japanese language has two sets of letters, known as *hiragana* and *katakana*, which are used to write some Japanese as well as foreign words. For example, the word *aisukuri-mu* comes from the English "ice cream."

Festivals

The Japanese enjoy following the changing seasons. TV weather reports feature maps showing where the spring blossoms and autumn leaves are at their best. Children especially enjoy summer festivals when holy shrines and streets are lined with stalls selling pancakes and cotton candy. After dark, spectators enjoy giant firework displays. During the festivals, some people wear a light summer version of Japan's traditional dress, the kimono. In winter, kimonos are worn in layers to provide more warmth.

▶ *Japanese men and women wear kimonos on special occasions, such as weddings and summer festivals. This is a Mother's Day celebration.*

Religion and Beliefs

When asked, most Japanese people say they follow both the main religions, Shintoism and Buddhism. These have existed alongside each other for over 1,500 years. However, religion does not play a big part in most people's lives. Many only visit shrines or temples on special occasions, such as the New Year. In Shinto, there is a belief that everything has a spiritual element, whether it is a tree, a stream, or a mountain. One form of Buddhism, Zen, is especially popular in Japan. Zen Buddhists believe in the power of meditation rather than following what is written in holy books.

GLOBAL LEADER

Working Hours

Japan has a reputation for being one of the hardest-working places in the world, but attitudes are changing slowly. Many large firms have officially adopted a five-day work week. However, many Japanese people still work late into the night or over the weekend for no extra pay. In 2002, the Japanese school week was also cut from six days to five, to give children more time off over the weekend.

Torii are gates at the entrances to Shinto shrines. This is the famous "floating torii," so called because when the tide is in, it seems to float on the water.

Growing Up in Japan

The school system in Japan is made up of elementary school (lasting six years), middle school (three years), high school (three years), and college (four years). Japanese children are expected to study very hard. They attend private lessons after school, known as *juku*, from a young age until they go to college. At school, classes are divided into small teams. Every day the teams take turns cleaning the classrooms, halls, and playing fields at school. Outside the classroom, baseball clubs, video games, *anime* (cartoons), and other TV shows are all very popular.

THE HOME OF...

Cartoons

Japanese *anime*, or animated shows, have been enjoyed by Japanese children since the 1960s. Series such as *Dragon Ball Z* and *Sailor Moon* are shown on TV all over the globe. Many shows, such as *Astro Boy*, are based on comic books, or *manga*. In 2003, Japanese *anime* director Miyazaki Hayao won the Oscar for Best Animated Feature for *Spirited Away*.

A Way of Life

Traditional crafts such as the Japanese tea ceremony and flower arranging are still part of the everyday lives of Japanese people. Both are influenced by Zen Buddhist ideas about living in harmony with nature and achieving inner calm. The tea ceremony involves preparing and serving green tea for guests. There are more than 20 schools of flower arrangement, or *ikebana*. Great care is taken with the choice of plants, the container, and how each branch and flower is placed.

▼ *The tea-maker in the tea ceremony tries to "live in the moment" to better appreciate the spiritual side of everyday life.*

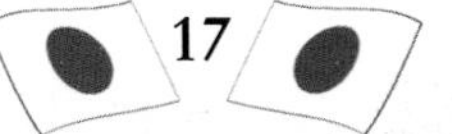

Music and Theater

Traditional Japanese music has changed little in 1,000 years, but folk songs are less popular now than they used to be. Young Japanese people listen to modern Japanese (J-pop) and Western pop songs. However, many traditional arts continue to thrive in Japan. *Kabuki* is a mix of music, theater, dance, and acrobatics performed by an all-male cast. *Noh* is musical theater performed by actors in masks, while *bunraku* is puppet theater accompanied by music. Japanese artists are also famous for their calligraphy and woodblock prints known as *ukiyo-e*.

In Japanese kabuki *theater, actors wear extravagant costumes and makeup. Mechanical devices are used to create special effects on stage.*

THE HOME OF...

Karaoke

Karaoke is a type of entertainment in which people sing along with recorded music, following the lyrics on a TV screen. Invented by the Japanese musician Daisuke Inoue in 1971, it became hugely popular during the 1990s when it spread to the rest of Asia and the United States. As well as singing at home, many Japanese people enjoy going to karaoke bars.

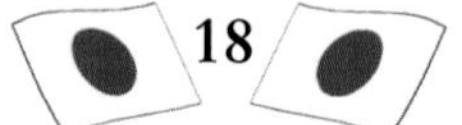

IT STARTED HERE

Sumo Wrestling

The martial art of Sumo wrestling started in Japan over 2,000 years ago. Two huge men, wearing only bellybands, try to force their opponent out of the ring or to the ground. Professional wrestlers live in "stables" where they follow strict traditions. They skip breakfast, but eat a very large lunch followed by a nap, which helps them to put on weight.

▲ *Sumo wrestlers line up before the Grand Sumo Tournament in Tokyo.*

Sports and Leisure

Many different sports are played in Japan. Traditional martial arts such as judo, karate, and kendo (Japanese fencing) are popular, as well as imported spectator sports such as football and baseball. Other interests include comic strips (*manga*) and *pachinko*, a sort of pinball with gambling. *Pachinko* arcades can be found in every Japanese town. Many Japanese enjoy surfing and scuba diving in the sea during summer, while skiing and snowboarding are popular winter sports.

Food and Drink

Although Western food such as hamburgers and bread are increasingly popular, traditional foods are an important part of Japanese life. White rice is eaten with all meals. Some of the accompanying fish, meat, and vegetable dishes are cooked, while others, such as *sashimi* (fish), are eaten raw. Popular dishes include *sushi* (sour rice dishes), *miso* soup, and *oden* (a stew). Beer is the most popular alcoholic drink in Japan along with the traditional rice wine called *sake*. Many young people enjoy gel-style health drinks or canned coffee.

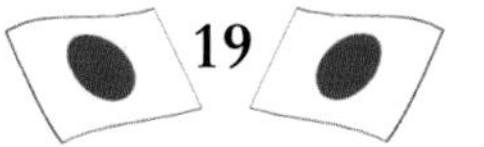

Economy and Trade

Japan's economy is the second-largest in the world and the most technologically advanced. Japanese electronic goods are sold all over the world. Although Japan imports most of its raw materials and much of its energy, it is also home to heavy industries such as steel and shipbuilding.

The Post-War Miracle

In the 1960s, the Japanese economy grew by 10 percent each year—an incredible achievement given that many of Japan's industries were destroyed in World War II. The growth was mainly achieved by exporting goods to the United States, which allowed Japan to buy foreign raw materials such as oil and iron ore. At the same time, Japan's farming industry shrank. Only 15 percent of the land in Japan is suitable for farming, and today Japan imports 60 percent of its food, much of it from China. Recently, the Japanese have also been buying more foreign goods, including computers and cars.

▼ *Customers look at the latest televisions in an electronics store in Tokyo.*

GLOBAL LEADER

Electronics

Japan is the largest consumer electronics manufacturer in the world. Japanese brands are known for their quality, style, and innovation, having created products such as Blu-ray disks and players.

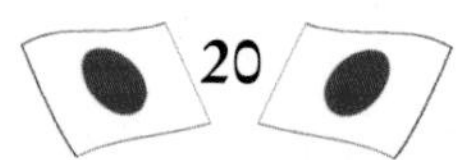

◀ *The Pivo 2 robot-assisted eco-car demonstrates Japan's use of cutting-edge technology to make products that are not available anywhere else in the world.*

Economic Slowdown

Japan's rapid growth ran out of steam in the 1990s, partly because the Japanese yen rose in value against the U.S. dollar, making Japanese goods more expensive overseas. Many Japanese firms moved their factories to countries where workers were paid less, such as China and Vietnam. However, soon firms in other Asian countries were producing their own goods even more cheaply. This forced Japanese companies to focus on unique, high-quality products using advanced technology, such as eco-cars. Despite this, exports of Japanese cars and other consumer goods were hit by the economic crisis that began in 2008.

IT STARTED HERE

Chindogu

***Chindogu* is the Japanese art of inventing everyday gadgets that appear ingenious but are impractical or embarrasing to use. One example is dusting slippers for cats, so they can help with the housework! The all-day tissue dispenser, for people suffering from hay fever, is simply a roll of toilet paper on top of a hat.**

Modern yet Traditional

Japan is a modern, highly developed country with high-tech communications and one of the best public transportation networks in the world. And yet, it remains a traditional society. Japanese men tend to work for the same employer throughout their working lives. Traditional attitudes about women at work still exist—just nine percent of managers in the workplace are women, and women are paid only two-thirds what men earn. Things are changing slowly, especially as Japan's aging population means more women are needed in the workforce.

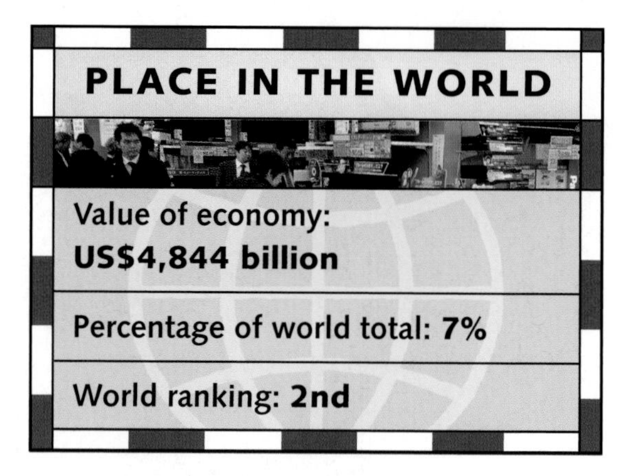

PLACE IN THE WORLD

Value of economy: **US$4,844 billion**

Percentage of world total: **7%**

World ranking: **2nd**

▼ *A woman sells cell phones in a store. Women hold few high-ranking positions in business in Japan.*

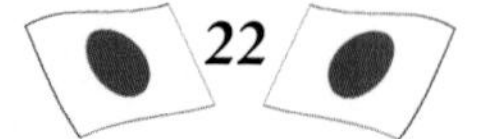

▲ *The Japanese "bullet trains" transport more than 150 million passengers a year.*

IT STARTED HERE

Bullet Trains

Japan was the first country to develop high-speed trains in 1964. These trains now run at speeds of up to 185 mph (300 km/h). The "bullet trains," or *shinkansen*, are also known for their standards of cleanliness, punctuality, and reliability.

Overseas Links

Japan is one of the world's great traders, so good relations with its overseas partners are very important. The Japanese government is an active member of the World Bank and the G8 group of the world's eight leading industrialized nations. Since the 1980s, it has been one of the world's most generous countries. In 2007, Japan donated US$7.7 billion to developing countries, especially those in Asia. It is also one of the world's largest overseas investors. Building factories overseas allows Japanese companies to take advantage of lower wages and to avoid restrictions on the import of overseas goods.

Competing with China

The balance of power is shifting in Asia as the Chinese economy grows and competes with Japan. Like Japan, China has a well-educated workforce, but its workers are paid much less. China's economy is also more open to foreign investment. However, both countries suffered as a result of the global economic crisis, and in 2008, the leaders of Japan, China, and South Korea agreed to work together to help solve Asia's economic problems.

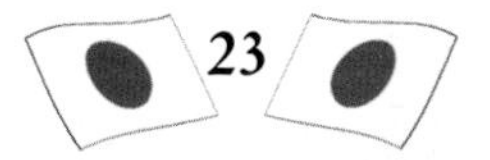

Government and Politics

During the first half of the 20th century, an emperor ruled Japan, but after the country's surrender at the end of World War II, Japan was governed by a democratic parliament, known as the Diet. Anyone over the age of 20 can vote, and the government is led by a prime minister. Although Japan still has an emperor, he has no political power.

FAMOUS JAPANESE

Toyotomi Hideyoshi (1536–98)

Hideyoshi was a Japanese general who united Japan in the 16th century, ending a bloody civil war that had lasted for over a century. He is also famous for building the elegant Osaka castle, which is a popular tourist destination still today.

The Japanese Empire

The history of modern Japan begins in 1868, when the Meiji emperor came back into power. The emperor allowed trade with the outside world for the first time in hundreds of years, and Japan began to modernize with help from foreign experts. After World War I (1914–18), Japan emerged as a major world power. In the 1930s it tried to expand its empire, invading Manchuria in 1931 and China in 1937. In 1941, Japan launched a surprise attack on the U.S. naval base at

◀ *The Meiji Shrine was built in memory of Emperor Meiji and his wife, Empress Shoken.*

Pearl Harbor. The Allies fought back, and in August 1945, the Americans dropped two atomic bombs on the Japanese cities of Hiroshima and Nagasaki, causing devastation.

The Japanese Parliament

After World War II, the Allies forced Japan to have a new constitution, giving more power to the parliament. Today, the Japanese parliament is made up of the House of Representatives and the House of Councillors, known together as the Diet. Although women have been able to vote in Japan since 1947, there are few women in government. In 2003, Japan ranked 97th in the world in terms of the number of female lawmakers.

THE HOME OF...

The Chrysanthemum Throne

The Japanese monarchy, known as The Chrysanthemum Throne, is the world's oldest ruling family. It has lasted for 2,600 years and the current emperor, Akihito, is the 125th emperor of Japan. Today's royal family has no real power and mainly performs ceremonial and social duties. Only men are allowed to rule. In 2006, a crisis over the monarchy's future was avoided when Princess Kiko gave birth to a boy—the first born in the family in 40 years.

▼ *Emperor Akihito and his wife Empress Michiko fill a mainly ceremonial role.*

Political and Legal System

The political system in Japan is based on those in the U.S. and Europe. Japan has an elected parliament, while its emperor is head of state. In 1896, the Japanese government created the *Minpo*, or Civil Code, which is based on the German and French systems of law. The Japanese constitution, introduced at the end of World War II, also includes a Bill of Rights similar to that in the U.S. Unlike many countries, the courts in Japan rarely use juries except for very serious crimes.

International Relations

Japan's new constitution in 1947 stated that the country would not fight in international wars, and for many years Japan's armed forces were not allowed overseas. Since 1992, however, they have been part of UN peacekeeping missions to countries such as Mozambique and East Timor. Japan's relations with its Asian neighbors China, Taiwan, and South Korea are still influenced by the harsh Japanese rule in these countries during the early 20th century.

▼ *The Japanese government meets in The National Diet Building in Tokyo.*

U.S. Military Support

At the end of World War II, U.S. forces remained in Japan for seven years. In 1960, Japan signed an alliance with the United States in which the U.S. promised to defend Japan with nuclear weapons if necessary. In recent years, some Japanese politicians have argued that Japan should take control of their own defense. However, nuclear missile tests in North Korea have become a big concern for the Japanese, so U.S. military support is likely to continue. In 2007, there were still over 33,000 U.S. troops based in Japan, and the Japanese port of Yokosuka is a base for the U.S. Seventh Fleet.

IT'S A FACT!

Japan has been a member of the UN since 1956. For many years it has argued for a permanent seat on the UN Security Council—the most important group within the United Nations—which would give it more influence in discussions on international conflicts and disputes.

▼ *The Japanese Self-Defense Force in Iraq in 2004. This was the first major overseas mission for Japanese soldiers since World War II.*

Japan in 2020

Japan has transformed itself over the past 50 years and there is every reason to believe it will remain a global economic power. Yet future Japanese governments will have to deal with the problems of global warming, an increasingly old population, and tough competition from economic rivals in Asia.

Going Digital

The Japanese government plans to make Japan a leader in digital technology with everything from toasters to toilets having microcomputers and sensors. It also hopes to increase the number of people who work from home using computers, known as telecommuters. A national fiber-optic network is already in place, giving Japan one of the fastest—and cheapest—broadband networks in the world. As in the United States, cell phones are already used in Japan to read newspapers or order tickets. In the future, video eyewear will allow cell-phone users to watch news, sports, and films anywhere, anytime,and they will even be able to send messages by blinking!

Japan leads the world in the field of robotics. ASIMO, a humanoid robot developed by Honda, can walk on two legs and speak human languages. It looks like an astronaut with a backpack.

Getting Older

Fewer and fewer Japanese people are choosing to have children. By 2020, Japan will have the oldest population of any industrial nation in the world. In 2007, 20 percent of Japan's population was 65 or over, making it the oldest society in human history. As its young workforce shrinks, Japan will need more foreign workers for its economy to grow. There will be fewer taxes to support the elderly. As young people head to the cities, many villages in the country could turn into ghost towns.

◀ *Child in traditional clothes. The birth rate in Japan is dropping as more couples are choosing to have only one child or none at all.*

Global Warming

In Japan, global warming is expected to bring more floods and landslides, more powerful typhoons, and more deaths from heatstroke. Despite this, Japan remains the world's fifth-biggest emitter of the greenhouse gases that contribute to global warming. Although there are plans to use more efficient cars and household machines, not much power currently comes from renewable energy sources. Just 1.65 percent of Japan's energy is expected to come from solar and wind power by 2014.

IT'S A FACT!

Thanks to global warming, parakeets and palm trees are increasingly common in Tokyo's sweltering concrete jungle, which is a little warmer than surrounding areas. One hundred years ago, there were just a few "tropical" nights each year, when temperatures did not drop below 77°F (25°C). By 2010 there were between 50 and 60 tropical nights.

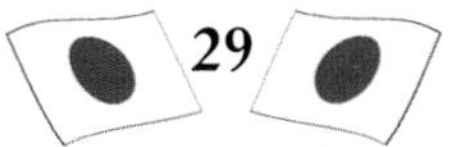

Glossary

bonsai the Japanese art of growing miniature trees and shrubs.

Buddhism an ancient religion that focuses on the teachings of the Buddha; founded in India.

civil war when two groups within a country fight each other.

constitution a document that lays out the main laws of a nation; laws are not allowed to be passed that contradict a country's constitution.

democratic a political system in which the people of a country choose their leaders through elections.

dialect the way a particular language is spoken in different parts of a country.

discrimination when someone is not allowed to do something or is considered less important than others because of their race or sex.

economy the financial system of a country or region, including how much money is made from the production and sale of goods and services.

emigrant someone who has left the country of their birth to settle in another country.

ethnic group a group of people classed together according to their racial, national, linguistic, or cultural origin or background.

export to send or transport products or materials abroad for sale or trade.

global warming the gradual rise in temperatures on the surface of the earth caused by changes in the amount of greenhouse gases in the atmosphere.

habitat a particular area where wildlife lives, such as a forest or a mountain.

hydroelectricity electricity generated by turbines that are turned by running water.

import to bring in goods or materials from another country for sale.

life expectancy the average number of years lived by a country's population.

monsoon a seasonal wind that blows in Asia; in the summer, monsoons bring rain to Japan.

peninsula a large mass of land that juts out into a body of water.

pollution ruining the environment with man-made waste such as chemicals or trash.

Shintoism an ancient Japanese religion based around ancestor worship.

typhoon a tropical cyclone in the Pacific or Indian oceans.

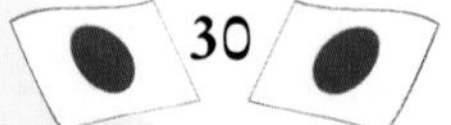

Further Information

Books

Japan
Celebrate!
by Robyn Hardyman
(Chelsea Clubhouse, 2009)

Japan
Welcome to My Country
by Harlinah White and Nicole Frank
(Marshall Cavendish Benchmark, 2010)

Japan
QEB Travel Through
by Joe Fullman
(QEB Publishing, 2007)

Japan: The Land
The Lands, Peoples, and Cultures
by Bobbie Kalman
(Crabtree Pub. Co., 2009)

Web Sites

http://cyberschoolbus.un.org/infonation/index.asp?theme=
The United Nations website about Japan.

http://www.jnto.go.jp/
Japan's National Tourism Organization website.

https://www.cia.gov/library/publications/the-world-factbook/geos/ja.html
The CIA's fact page of Japan featuring maps and brief descriptions of the land, people, government, and economy.

http://web-japan.org/kidsweb/
Just for kids, this site introduces the country, its people, language, culture, and history.

Every effort has been made by the publisher to ensure that these web sites contain no inappropriate or offensive material. However, because of the nature of the Internet, it is impossible to guarantee that the content of these sites will not be altered. We strongly advise that Internet access is supervised by a responsible adult.

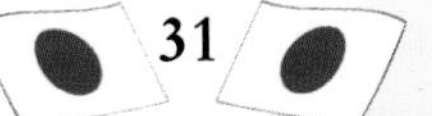

Index

Numbers in **bold** indicate pictures